Travelling A
The Isle (

on old pictur

Andrew Swift

MR. & MRS. GODFREY BARING, AT BEMBRIDGE. ISLE OF WIGHT. JANUARY. 1906.

1. The appearance of this new-fangled motor car in the middle of **Bembridge** early in 1906 probably caused as much excitement as the identity of its occupants. At the time there were only around 10,000 cars in the entire country and the numberplate on Mr Baring's car - DL 82 - gives an idea of how many vehicles there were on the Island. The car, which has unusually protruding axle hubs and self-generating acetylene headlamps, may be a Panhard. Mr Baring, who lived at Nubia House, Cowes, was elected as Liberal MP for the Island in January 1906, the month this photograph was taken, thus ending 25 years of Conservative rule. The shop in the background, Mr Couldrey's Emporium, is now Watson, Bull & Porter's Estate Agents. *FN Broderick*

£3.50

2. A horse-drawn carriage climbing Binstead Hill - today part of the A3054 from Ryde to Newport. By today's standards it is astonishingly empty. But personal transport was far from being the norm in 1905, when this picture was taken. Only the rich had horse-drawn carriages and there were fewer than 100 cars on the Island. Everybody else had to walk, take the train or, if they were lucky, climb on one of the new-fangled cycles. If you'd have told them that, a hundred years hence, there'd be out-of-town supermarkets, roads clogged with cars and roll on, roll off ferries every half hour just up the road at Fishbourne, they'd have said you were talking through your exhaust. *FN Broderick*

INTRODUCTION

When the poet Edward Thomas came to the Island in 1911 to write a travel book he found *"the only inconveniences"* to be *"the bad and expensive railways and the other people."* Little did he think that less than a century later the Isle of Wight Steam Railway would be one of the Island's foremost attractions.

People - Thomas's other *"inconvenience"* - are still in much in evidence on the Island, as we will find if we attempt to drive through Sandown or Shanklin in mid-August or to find a parking spot in Cowes during Cowes Week. But the network of railways - all except for the electrified stretch from Ryde to Shanklin and the steam railway at Havenstreet - has gone. Much of it went in the 1950s and by the time the last steam train was withdrawn in 1966 what was left was a museum piece. But as a museum piece it had many admirers.

It is a fair guess that more books have been written about the Island's railways than about any other system of comparable size anywhere. The steamers and ferries that ran to and from the mainland are also well documented. But other forms of transport - the buses, cars and horse-drawn carriages which once rattled along the roads - are comparatively neglected. Although this small book covers some of the ground that has been gone over - in much greater detail - in the many books on the Island's railways, it also includes postcards showing the other means people used to get around early last century. So forget about the exhaust fumes hanging in the air, the queues of traffic clogging the lanes and the lack of parking spaces and look back to a time when the hedgerows were white with dust, when traffic pollution doubled as manure for the roses and a traffic hold-up was two people having a chat in the middle of the road.

Andrew Swift
April 2000

3. The first bus services on the Isle of Wight started on 13 April 1905. Four buses were brought over to the Island and after the opening ceremony on Ryde Esplanade they set off for Bembridge, Cowes, Newport and Shanklin. The unpopularity of the Island's trains fuelled the enthusiastic welcome given to the buses. The optimism was, however, short-lived. The buses couldn't cope with the hills and before the year was out they were withdrawn and replaced by single-deckers. These were only marginally more successful and were gone within a couple of years. Not until the early 1920's, when their design and reliability had improved, did buses once again appear on the Island's roads. *FN Broderick*

4. The Bembridge bus outside Mr Couldrey's emporium. *"Had a strawberry feed at Mrs Fardell's today - quite enjoyed it,"* runs the message on this card sent to Portsmouth on 2 July 1907. And everything has stopped for the photographer. Mr Couldrey - the man with the Elgarian moustache on the right - has come out of his shop. In the distance a farm worker stands holding a half-open gate while his horse waits patiently with a laden cart. Note the registration of the bus - DL 80 - just two before Mr Baring's car. *FN Broderick*

5. A view of Ryde Pier from around 1905. The rail link from St John's Road Station to the Pier Head opened in 1880. It was built, not by any of the Island's railway companies, but by two mainland companies - the London & South Western and the London, Brighton & South Coast - which were keen to develop services to the Isle of Wight. Even before the first pier at Ryde opened in 1814, Ryde was the favourite place to arrive on the Island. By the time the railway pier opened, it had no real competition until the growth of private motoring and the introduction of car ferries to Fishbourne, East Cowes and Lymington.

11   RYDE (Isle of Wight). — The Pier. — The Pavilion. — LL.

6. One of the electric tramcars which operated on Ryde Pier between 1886 and 1927 on a card sent to Newport on 2 June 1906. The leading car appears to be the famous Grapes Car of 1867 (so called because it was decorated with carvings of grapes) which started life as a double-decked horse tram and eventually became a petrol car trailer when the pier tramway was de-electrified. Withdrawn after an argument with the buffer stops in 1935, it was bought privately, restored, and is now in Hull Museum. *LL*

7. The Southern Railway, which operated the ferry service from Lymington to Yarmouth Pier, introduced its first car ferry - the *Lymington* - on this route in 1938. It docked at the quay instead of the pier and a new slipway was built. This view of **Yarmouth** dates from the 1950's. *Nigh of Ventnor*

8. An early roll-on, roll-off ferry at Fishbourne, although in this case rolling seems the wrong metaphor. More like 'One Man and His Pig.' Aubrey de Selincourt wrote of this ferry in 1948, " *two or three times a day she noses her way in past the Dolphins and ties up in the little basin below the point. She is a queer monster - like a sort of hippopotamus - turns in her own length, and goes forward or backwards, and I believe sideways, with equal facility." Raphael Tuck & Sons*

CHAIN PIER, SEA VIEW, I. O. W.

23

9. In the latter half of the nineteenth century, the tourist trade boomed and resorts all round the Island vied with each other to attract visitors. The best way to do this was to build a pier so that steamers could bring passengers directly from the mainland. Between 1841 and 1890 piers were built at Cowes, Ventnor, Yarmouth, Sandown, Totland Bay, Seaview, Alum Bay and Shanklin and they all had regular steamer services to and from the mainland. Most have now gone. Perhaps the saddest loss was the suspension pier at Seaview, seen here on a card sent to Loughton around 1930, with passengers joining one of the second generation of Isle of Wight buses to go to Ryde. The inconvenience of having to rely on vehicles such as this must have made steamers an attractive alternative.

THE PIER, COWES, I.W. D.1019.

10. This card showing the Victoria Pier at **Cowes** was sent to Stockton on Tees on 18 September 1957, although the photograph dates from before 1951 when the pavilion was demolished. This was the third pier to be built at Cowes and dated from 1902. It was demolished in the early 1960's. *Deans of Sandown*

Totland Bay, I.W.

norman sends his love and says he would also a walking stick for Xmas. Many thanks for letter – Reading Room, Hotel & steamer we came in. Much love, yours Fanny

11. This card of Totland Bay Pier was sent to Bedford on 19 November 1902: *"Norman sends his love and says he would like a walking stick for Xmas."* Bathing huts tethered to the shore, a steamer calling at the pier - the epitome of the Edwardian seaside resort. Totland Bay is still unspoiled today and, although the hotel on the cliffs has gone, the pier is still there. At present it is closed because it is unsafe, but there are hopes that it can be restored to its former glory.

12. Another view of **Ryde** on a card showing an alternative to the ferry - the early air service from Portsmouth. St John's Road Station can be seen to the left of the photo, and the course of the railway can be followed until it disappears into the tunnel to the right and re-emerges to run along the pier.

13. Bembridge Station in the early years of the twentieth century. It looked quaint eve
of this card, sent to London on 4 August 1911. *"All the time it is in the station it is puffir
is right). How's your tortoise getting on? Love Mabel."* Talk about association of ideas! Th
lines, but today picture postcards like this convey a sense of something irreparably los
Wilson of Bembridge

WILSON. 69.

en. "This is the express that runs to Brading and back," reads the message on the back
ost tremendously. It is very busy just now - seems as if it had asthma (Hope the spelling
75 mile Bembridge branch was, in its lifetime, one of the most derided of the Island's
embridge Station closed on 21 September 1953 and today all trace of it has disappeared.

14. Ryde St John's Road Station early last century with the old railway works in the background. From 1864 to 1880 this was the northern terminus of the Isle of Wight Railway. Passengers who wanted the ferry to the mainland had to make their way to the pier by horse-drawn carriage or - from 1871 - by horse-drawn tram. Not until 16 years after St John's Road opened was the line extended to the Pier Head.

15. Inside the signalbox at **Ryde St John's Road** in 1949. Since the closure of the box at Sandown in 1988, the box at St John's Road has been the centralised control point for the entire line between Ryde and Shanklin. *AG Ellis*

16. The first station south of St John's Road is Brading. On this card dating from 1913 *Bonchurch* is in charge of a set of rather rickety-looking coaches. When *Bonchurch* came over to the Island in 1883 the barge carrying her sank off St Helen's. She was eventually recovered by being dragged along the seabed until she reached low water mark, at which point rails were laid across the sands to haul her onto dry land. After a spell in Ryde Works she emerged as good as new. By the time she was withdrawn in 1928 she had worked 1,326,067 miles on the Island. *F Moore*

17. From 1882 to 1953 Brading was the junction for the Bembridge branch. The only intermediate station on the branch was at **St Helen's**, seen here in Southern Railway days. After the line closed the station building was turned into a private house. *HC Casserley*

18. When the railway reached Sandown in 1864, it was no more than a village, but within three years an esplanade had been built, and villas and hotels were springing up everywhere. So fast was its growth that in 1875 another line was opened from Newport to Sandown. In this view from between the wars a train for Ventnor climbs out of Sandown. This original line through Sandown is still open but the Newport-Sandown branch closed in 1956.

19. Shanklin station opened in 1864 as the terminus of the line from Ryde. Like Sandown, Shanklin was little more than a village when the railway arrived. Two years later the line was extended to Ventnor. The Shanklin-Ventnor section closed in 1966 and today Shanklin is once again the end of the line and the platform on the right is the only one in use.

20. Wroxall was the only intermediate station between Shanklin and Ventnor. Aubrey de Selincourt, writing in 1948, thought the station the most attractive feature of the village, *"where on one side the platform is backed by a sloping cabbage rose patch dotted with apple trees and fine clumps of purple mallow and climbing roses."* The line closed in 1966 and the site of the station is now occupied by an industrial estate.

21. The station at **Ventnor** was a delight. Seen from high above it looked like a model, scooped out of the side of the hill into which the trains disappeared as soon as they left the platform. But although St Boniface Down loomed over it, it was still 294 feet above sea level, as a notice board on the platform informed alighting passengers. Over the years there were many plans to link the station with the town centre and sea front by tramway or cliff railway but these came to nothing and the line closed in 1966.

22. Over thirty years after the first railway reached Ventnor another opened in competition. This branched off the Newport-Sandown line at Merstone and ran to a station in the grounds of Steephill Castle about a mile from Ventnor town centre. There were three intermediate stations - Godshill, Whitwell and St Lawrence. This is **Godshill**, where a note in a timetable from 1910 informed passengers that *"the train stops to take up on giving notice at the station, and sets down on the passenger informing the guard at the previous stopping station."*

23. After burrowing through a tunnel south of Whitwell the line emerged at St Lawrence, on a high ledge cut into the Undercliff. The station at **St Lawrence** frequently suffered from rock falls, as this card from 1903 shows. John Betjeman travelled on this line just after the Second World War and left us this description of the final stretch from St Lawrence to Ventnor: *"Sycamores and ash trees wave above us and below us, old man's beard and bind-weed clamber over broken stone walls, damp-looking drives wind down to empty stables and huge houses turned into holiday camps are left to ghosts and centipedes, and all the time, between the ash-tree branches, an unexpected silver, shines the sea. If the Southern Railway had any sense it would put observation cars on this part of its system."*

24. A single-coach train stands at the empty platform at **Ventnor West**, the terminus of the line from Merstone. Despite John Betjeman's suggestion observation cars were not introduced on this line, which closed in 1952.

25. Alverstone Station, on the Newport-Sandown line, which opened in 1875 and closed in 1956. In this card from shortly after the First World War there are plenty of passengers waiting as a Sandown-bound train pulls in. The station building at Alverstone, like the other three stations on these two pages, is now a private house.

26. In 1889 the Freshwater, Yarmouth & Newport Railway Company opened a line from Newport to Freshwater. The line was operated from the start by the Isle of Wight Central Railway Company and trains had to reverse into the station at **Newport**. In this card from around 1905 the Isle of Wight Central Railway Company's loco no.11 is seen propelling a train into the Freshwater bay platform at Newport.

27. In 1913 the Freshwater, Yarmouth & Newport Company fell out with the Isle of Wight Central Railway, brought two locomotives over from the mainland to work its own services (see photo no. 32), built its own station at **Newport** - seen here around 1920 - and bankrupted itself in the process. It nevertheless managed to keep going until 1923 when all the Island's railways were absorbed by the Southern Railway. The Southern closed the separate station at Newport and trains went back to reversing into the main station until the branch closed in 1953.

28. First station out of Newport on the Freshwater line was **Carisbrooke**, seen here with an Isle of Wight Central train. In its early days it was very busy, especially in summer, with visitors to Carisbrooke Castle. The introduction of buses and coach tours in the 1920's effectively killed this traffic and in the years leading up to closure in 1953 it saw few passengers. Today all trace of the station has disappeared.

29. One of the main incentives for building a line to Freshwater was to develop the Lymington-Yarmouth ferry route. The Lymington Pier branch on the mainland had opened in 1884 and it is interesting to speculate what would have happened if a similar station had been built at Yarmouth, with fast rail connections to other parts of the Island. But the Freshwater, Yarmouth & Newport Company never really got their act together. Their station at **Yarmouth** was half a mile inland from the pier and the line never developed beyond a rural backwater. It closed in 1953.

30. The ultimate way for well-bred ladies to get around **Ryde** in the Edwardian era was i
from Aix-le-Bains in France with her in 1887 and harnessed it up to a carriage to draw he
1906, a little ensemble is seen outside the Waverley Hotel on Ryde Esplanade.

WAVERLEY HOTEL &
BOARDING ESTABLISMENT.

Meals Provided for Non Residents
at Reasonable Charges.

Boarding Terms

onkey cart. No less an Isle of Wight resident than Queen Victoria brought a donkey back
nd the grounds of Osborne House. On this card, sent to St Trond in Belgium on 10 May

REBUILT TRAIN FOR BEMBRIDGE BRANCH SERVICES

31. When the Southern Railway took over the Island's railways in 1923 they set about improving the services. Top of the agenda was the rolling stock in use on some of the branch services. "Museum piece" was not a term of approval in those far-off days, but that's what much of the Island's rolling stock undoubtedly was. This photo, dates from 1930, when *Fishbourne* - the locomotive shown at the head of these two coaches - came over to the Island. It was taken just outside St John's Road station in Ryde. Wood & Co's. coal yard is in the background.

32. Until Medina Wharf was extended in the 1920's, the main commercial docks on the Island were at **St Helen's.** In this card dating from 1913, LSWR No. 734 - one of the two locomotives brought over from the mainland by the Freshwater, Yarmouth & Newport Railway after its split with the Isle of Wight Central Railway - is seen being unloaded at St Helen's Docks, along with five coaches.

33. Engines were also offloaded at **Ryde Pier**. In this view dating from 1923 Ryde Pier Head Station can be seen in the background as an ex-London & South Western tank engine is lowered into position. After a visit to the works at St John's Road this locomotive emerged as No. 20 *Shanklin.*

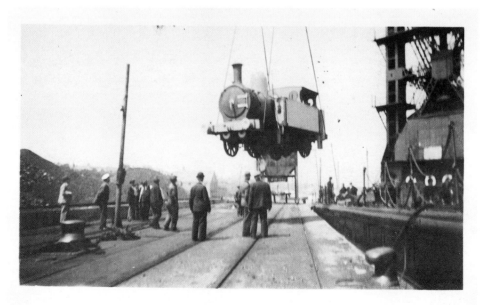

34. In later years **Medina Wharf** near Cowes was the usual point of entry and departure for locomotives and rolling stock. On this card, *Ryde,* built in 1864 and withdrawn from stock in 1932, is seen returning to the mainland in June 1934.

Isle of Wight Railway.

SHANKLIN.
3½ hours from London by express trains.

SHANKLIN CHINE.

35. In the early 1900's all four of the Island's railway companies - the Freshwater, Yarmouth & Newport Railway, the Isle of Wight Railway, the Isle of Wight Central Railway, and the Newport, Godshill & St Lawrence Railway - sold cards advertising their respective lines. This card, sent from Shanklin to New York on 5 May 1900, shows Shanklin Chine: *"Got this card at the Rail Station. Shall send you one every chance I get."*

36. *"Shanklin: 3½ hours from London by express trains,"* runs the slogan on the "official" railway card at the top of the page. Most people's perception of the Island's railways at the time, however, was closer to that expressed in this comic card published by Cynicus of Leeds and sent to Leamington Spa in 1915.

37. The reality of travel for most people on the Island 100 years ago was walking, as in this view of Church Street, **Havenstreet**, sent to Hastings on 11 July 1911. There were no buses and if the train didn't go where you wanted to go - or when - and you didn't own a horse or a bicycle, there was no alternative. *FN Broderick.*

38. We are so used to seeing bicycles these days that it is difficult to realise how fashionable and modern-looking they were in 1905 when this view of Chapel Road, **Binstead,** was sent to Uxbridge in Middlesex. This farmhand must have felt quite a swell - to coin a good old Edwardian term - following the cows on his bike. *FN Broderick*

39. The splendid sight of a coach and four rounding the corner at the top of Culver Parade in **Sandown** in 1907. Comfortable it almost certainly wasn't, but an outside seat on a coach like this would have been a superb way of getting around the Island on a warm summer's day. *FN Broderick*

40. Charabancs line up outside the Pier Hotel at **Ryde** in the 1920's with one or two horse-drawn carriages still hanging around in the background. It looks almost like a film set for Jeeves and Wooster. This card was sent to Market Deeping, Lincs. on 23 June 1927: *"We went to Shanklin and Ventnor Wednesday and Thursday we are going Newport & Carisbrooke & Newchurch. The time has gone quickly."*

41. A horse and cart rolls down Church Road in **Gurnard**. *"Rew Street Farm 17/9/06,"* reads the message on the back of this card, sent to Miss Hamilton at Stratton Villa in Glanville Road, Cowes. *"Dear Mabel, The blackberries are now ripe. Shall be pleased to see you on Thursday afternoon, if not fine can you come on Friday. With love from May."* FN Broderick

42. What better way to pass a few hours than to tie your horse up outside the Crab and Lobster on the Foreland at **Bembridge** and down a few pints of Mew Langton's in convivial company? And no worries about being over the limit when the time came to bid a fond farewell. After all, the horse could find its own way home - and if you were lucky it'd wait for you. The Crab & Lobster is still there today, much extended, and with, as its name suggests, a reputation for seafood. And - something not envisaged when this card was published - a large car park. *Photochrom of London.*

43. *"Thought you would like this card - just out,"* runs the message on this card sent to Three Bridges in Sussex on 29 February 1908. A meet of the Isle of Wight Foxhounds at the Grange, **Wootton**, home of Ernest Langton. A scene which could be recreated today, the difference being that back then horses were still part of everyday life, just as they had been for thousands of years. Only in the latter part of the twentieth century was man's - or in this case woman's - bond with and reliance on the horse consigned to the dustbin of history. *FN Broderick*

44. A officer of the law keeps watch over proceedings as a carriage draws up for a hunt meet at **Brading** in 1909. Despite the looks of apprehension on the faces of these hunt followers, they had little to worry about. Hunt saboteurs were not even a dot on a distant horizon. And the idea that one day the government would propose legislation to outlaw hunting with hounds would have seemed laughable. *FN Broderick*

45. The height of elegance at a hunt meet at **Carisbrooke** on 5 February 1909. Legs wrapped in furs, whip in hand and cigarette firmly in mouth. Just think how much dust he could stir up in one of these. *FN Broderick*

46. When it came to stirring up dust though, motor cars were the business. And by 1911 they were even getting to hunt meetings, as this Austin parked in a rather cavalier fashion at **East Standen** shows. This car DL 338 was registered in the Isle of Wight in 1906. The speed limit was 20 mph at this time, although motorists often exceeded it. During a debate on speed limits in the House of Lords an Irish Peer spoke for the road lobby when he argued that it was ridiculous to expect a vehicle travelling downhill to observe a speed limit. The driver of the car, with his car club cap badge and goggles tucked in the top pocket of his driving jacket, is on the left. *FN Broderick*

47. 1911 again - and a Hunt Meet at **Sheat Corner**. This time, internal combustion eng[
features. It has an AA badge and a personalised griffin mascot. Its headlights are acetyl[
section of the car may have been detachable, thus allowing the rear section to be use[
above the running board. This was an exhaust whistle, which was used instead of - o[
exhaust gases into the whistle and produced a "toot-toot-toot" sound which must h[
The car on the right - with a London registration - is a covered landaulette wit[

ORNER. MARCH 28, 1911

umber horses two to one. The vehicle on the left - a Daimler - has several interesting
ered by a generator on the running board. The fold-down step suggests that the back
y a shooting party or for some similar purpose. But most interesting is the brass pipe
as - a horn to warn of the car's approach. The driver operated a control which diverted
e wonders for scattering chickens.
cularly fine set of opera lights on either side of the bonnet. *FN Broderick*

48. Once again it's the car which is the star of this view of a hunt meet at **Yarmouth**. Registered in Southampton (CR) in 1906-07, it is seen outside the Royal Solent Yacht Club. At this time - and for many years to come - getting a car from the mainland was not a matter of "roll on, roll off" but of cranes and ships' holds. Although the make of the car cannot be determined, one noteworthy feature is the large dust-proof hood at the back - something that the well-dressed ladies in the back seat were no doubt grateful for. Note also the care with which the driver has wrapped the rear light in an oil cloth to keep it clean. *FN Broderick*

49. No double yellow lines in this view of an impressive early tourer - probably a Delauney Belleville - parked in the Old Village at **Shanklin**. This card was sent to London in 1912. It is impossible to conceive how much freedom early motorists had. But there was a down side to this freedom. People were used to having ownership of the roads. They wandered about in them at will, stopped and chatted when and where they wanted, and let their children play in them without a second thought. As a result fatalities in the early years of motoring were - considering the small number of cars on the road - horrendous. People learnt quickly and surrendered the roads to the cars. We may be infinitely more mobile than our Edwardian forebears but the freedom of the road - to wander when and where we will - has gone forever. *G & H Ancell of Sandown*

0. Another car, this time a Model T Ford with an Isle of Wight registration, parked across from e Post Office in **Whitwell** (now a private house) around the time of the First World War. Its umberplate - DL1562 - indicates that it was registered in 1909-10. However, the writer Audrey e Selincourt recalls that when he first came to Niton in 1919, *"there was nobody in it who wned a motor of any kind, car or van. We drove from Whitwell Station in a horse-drawn fly."*

1. Bicycles still outnumber cars two to one on this card of Small Hope Point at **hanklin** which was sent to Leicester on 2 August 1949. This Austin 7 Saloon has a orkshire registration and dates from around 1931. Choice of parking spaces by the ea on a sunny day like this are, sadly, but a distant memory.

52. Cycle power at **Havenstreet**. Two young men pause in the lane while the stationmaster, in lull between trains, stands on the path leading to the station. The station, on the line from Ryd to Newport, opened on 20 December 1875, and originally had a single platform. In 1926, as par of its effort to improve services, the Southern Railway built a loop for trains to cross a Havenstreet, with tracks running either side of the platform. The line closed on 21 February 196 but reopened as the headquarters of the Isle of Wight Steam Railway in 1971. This card date from around 1907 when Mr Deadman was stationmaster here. *FN Broderick*

53. Cycles at the **Seagrove Bay** Sports Day. This photo was taken on 17 August 1907. Th Sunlight Almanac for 1899 gave the following advice to young ladies eager to take up the ne cycling craze: *"To pedal properly, the ball of the foot must rest squarely on the pedal, followir the pedal on the downward stroke by bending the ankles, and catching it again as it ascend Beginners sometimes fail to keep up this crank motion, forgetting that to cease pedalling w cause the machine to topple over."* FN Broderick

4. The military joined the cycle craze, too, as this card of the Isle of Wight Rifles at their summer camp at **Yaverland** in 1909 shows. Scenes like this are a reminder how unprepared for the realities of modern warfare the British Army was in the years leading up to the outbreak of war in 1914. *FN Broderick*

5. The staff of Arthur Blackburn's grocery and coal merchants stand outside the shop to watch the 2nd Wessex Howitzer Brigade climbing Union Street in **Ryde**. When the First World War broke out, the British Army was still almost totally dependent on horse power. The Expeditionary Force which went to France in 1914 took 53,000 horses with them - against a mere 80 motor vehicles. Nobody was prepared for the impasse of trench warfare. As Lord French, the British Commander in Chief, later admitted, *"all my thoughts were concentrated upon a war of movement and manoeuvre."* *FN Broderick*

56. In the last week of October 1909 the Island suffered nearly a week of continuous rain. On th morning of Tuesday the 25th the 391 yard rail tunnel at **Ryde** was flooded to such an extent th. trains had to be cancelled. And still the rain continued. Sandown and Shanklin sent their fir engines to help the Ryde brigade pump out the water. Even Ryde's old manual engine wa pressed into service. But against this Noah's Ark style downpour they stood little chance. *F Broderick*

57. Not until this mighty "pulsometer" engine was brought in from Knighton Wate Works on Thursday the 27th did the level start to drop. Even then it was not until th following Monday morning that trains began running again. It was later estimate that around 7.5m gallons of water were pumped out of the tunnel. *FN Broderick*

58. A familiar figure on the dusty roads of England until well into the twentieth century was the carrier who transported goods between specified towns on certain days of the week. Here a carrier passes the Red Lion Inn in the otherwise empty High Street at **Brading.** Apart from the increase in traffic, this scene has hardly altered today, except for the demolition of some houses on the right to make way for a car park next to the Bugle Inn. *FN Broderick*

59. A horse and cart clatters along New Road, **Brading** on a card sent to Daisy Redstone of High Street, Brading on 11 August 1905. *"Dearest Daisy, I am now taking the liberty of sending your brother's photograph, Dinkie." FN Broderick*

THE UNDERCLIFF, WINDY CORNER, I.W.
BEFORE AND AFTER THE LANDSLIDE, JULY, 1926

60. *"This is one of our photos,"* reads the message on the back of this card, sent to Bishop Auckland on 10 October 1910. *"Will send you one of the others when I get it. This is my mate who cycled with me from Leicester."* The setting is the famous scenic stretch of road along the **Undercliff**.

61. The road along the Undercliff was buried under a massive rock fall on 26 July 1926 as this "before and after" card shows. A further landslip a couple of months later carried away the remains of the road and it never reopened.

62. On this card, sent from Ventnor on 26 June 1932 the new road is seen under construction well away from the site of the rock fall.